WHEN MOMMY DROPS ME OFF AT SCHOOL

Written by - ROSEANNE HINCH

ISBN: 979-8-218-47697-7

Printed in United states of America First Addition 7/2024.

DEDICATION

To all of my Grandchildren.
Keep being brave even when you don't think you can,

YOU CAN!

- Roseanne Hinch - AKA - Nawney

ABOUT THE AUTHOR

Author Roseanne Hinch is a first time author who lives in Abingdon, Maryland.

She runs a small licensed childcare business for the past 28 years.

Approximately 90 babies have been cared for and nurtured over the years.

Inspiring and helping your little learners with separation anxiety.

I know I have fun when I am at school,
I play with my friends and I follow the rules.

When it is time to say goodbye to mommy at the door, my eyes start to water, and it drips on the floor.

I try to be brave, for I miss my mommy so,
I don't want to be sad;
I dont wan't my mommy to go.

Page No - 7

When mommy goes,
and I see all my friends.

My eyes start to dry up,
and my heart is happy again.

I know I'll see my mommy,
when my school day is done.

I can tell her about all of the things,
that were, oh, so much fun!

She is always right there,
at the end of the day.

I put my coat on,
and I'm on my way.

Tomorrow when I go to school,
I'm going to be big and brave.

I'll bring in a picture of my family to looK at and save.

I'll remember that school is fun
and I learn more everyday,

I can share my day with mommy,
In the car along the way.

Page No – 19

www.ingramcontent.com/pod-product-compliance
Lightning Source LLC
Chambersburg PA
CBHW041458120626
46547CB00003B/474

WHEN DADDY DROPS ME OFF AT SCHOOL

Written by - ROSEANNE HINCH

I know I have fun when I am at school,
I play with my friends and I follow the rules.

When it is time to say goodbye to daddy at the door, my eyes start to water, and it drips on the floor.

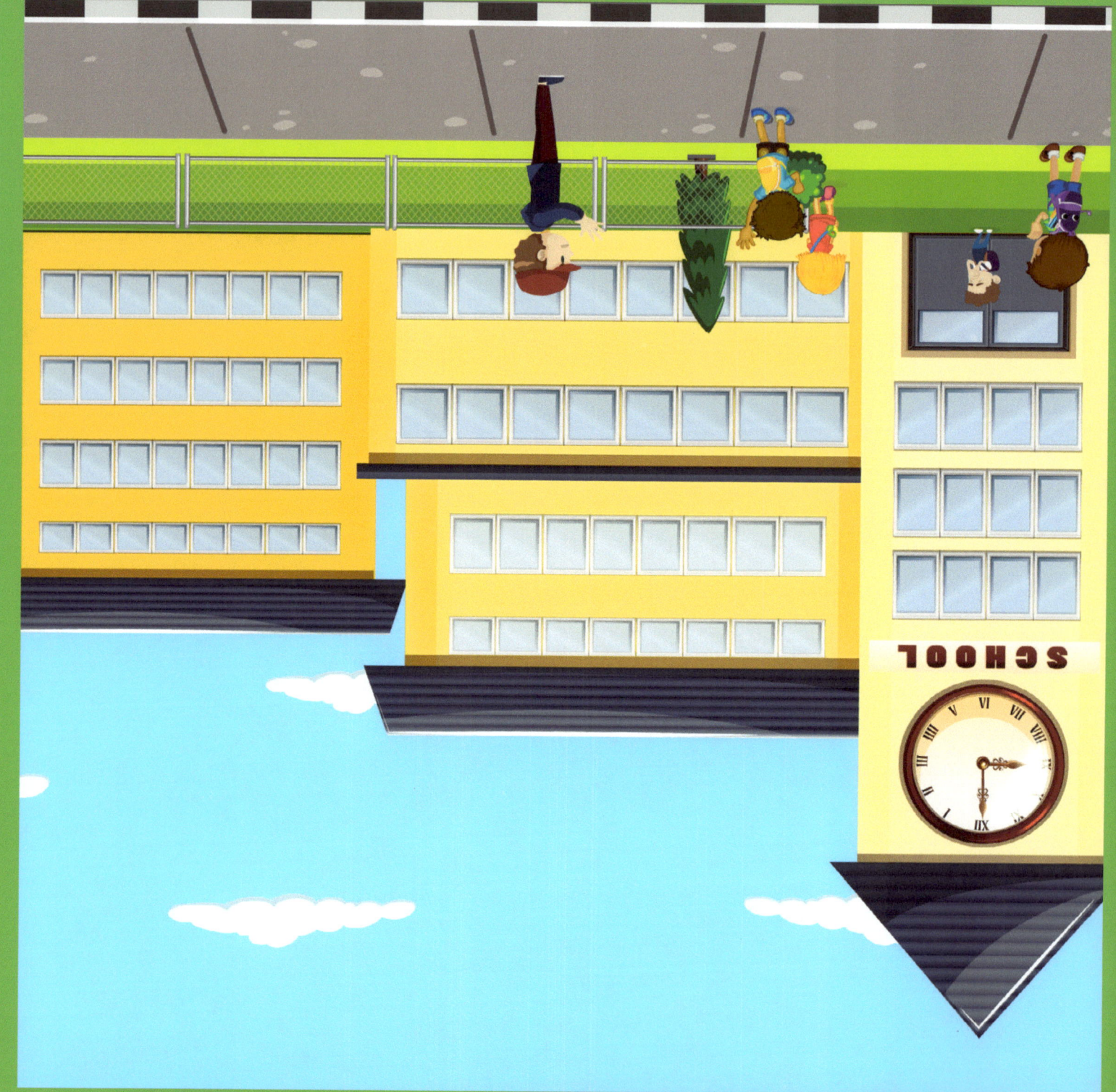

I try to be brave, for I miss my daddy so.
I don't want to be sad;
I dont want my daddy to go.

My eyes start to dry up,
and my heart is happy again.

When daddy goes,
and I see all my friends.

I know I'll see my daddy,
when my school day is done.

I can tell him about all of the things,
that were, oh, so much fun!

He is always right there,
at the end of the day.

I put my coat on,
and I'm on my way.

Tomorrow when I go to school,
I'm going to be big and brave.

I'll bring in a picture of my family to looK at and save.

Page No – 15

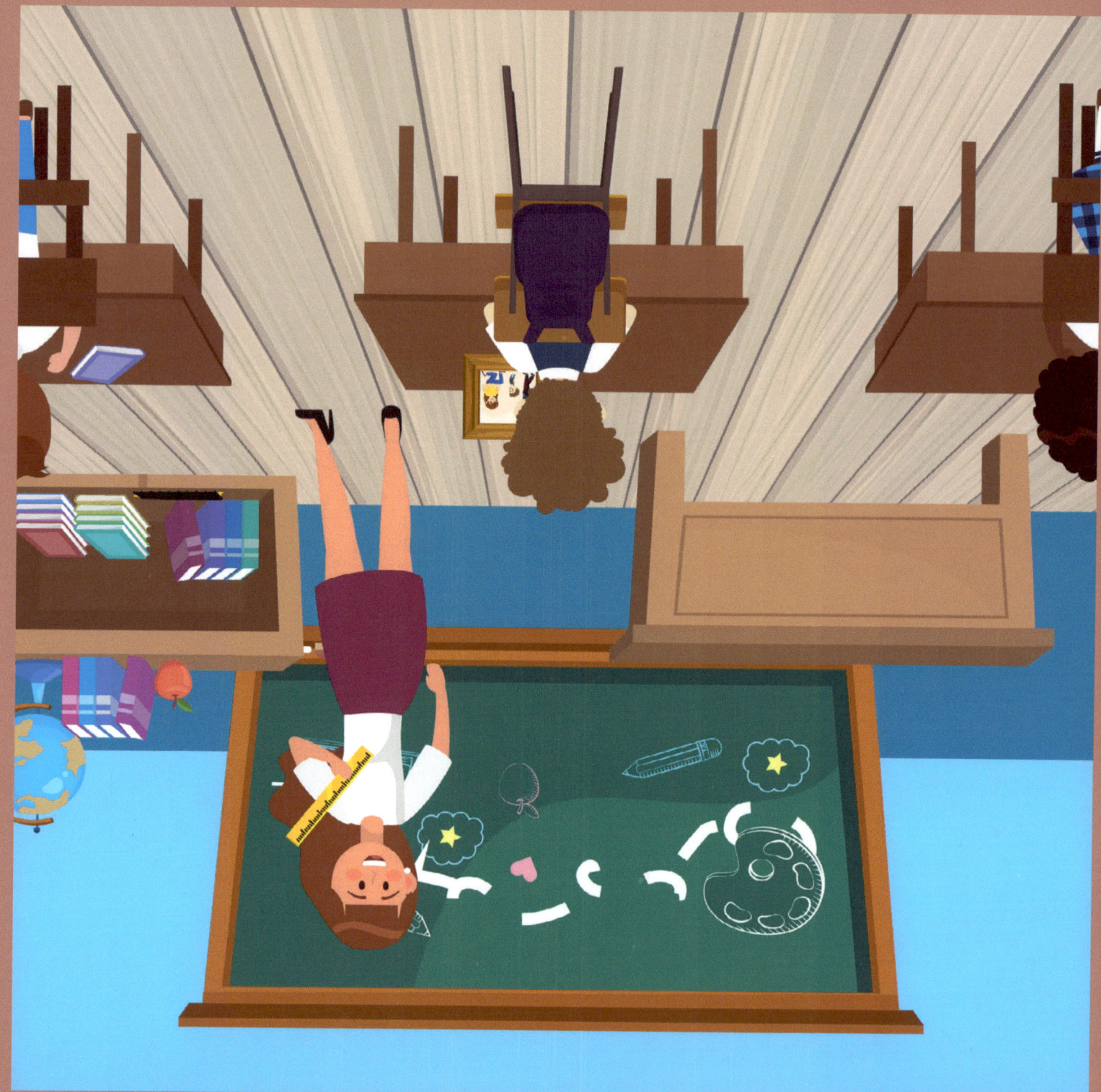

I'll remember that school is fun
and I learn more everyday,

I can share my day with daddy,
In the car along the way.

When Daddy drops me off
at school it may be scary.
Learning how to be brave.

Knowing I'll share my day with him on our way home. Helping children with separation anxiety.

Knowing I'll share my day with her on our way home. Helping children with separation anxiety.

When Mommy drops me off at school it may be scary. Learning how to be brave,

MY FRIENDS

MY FAMILY

FIRST DAY AT SCHOOL

MY BUS

MY LUNCH

MY CLOTHES

How much I missed my parents

How I managed to get through the day

How I cope up with my anxiety

_____

_____

_____

_____

_____

_____

My first day at school